11070055

NO LONGER PROPERTY
KING COUNTY LIBRARY SYSTEM

FEB - - 2008

Read and Play
Trains

by Jim Pipe

Stargazer Books

train

2

Here is a **train**.

A **train** pulls a big load.

3

engine

4

A train has a strong **engine**.

driver

A train has a **driver**.

5

wheels

6

A train has **wheels**.

Wheels roll around.

7

tracks

8

A train runs on **tracks**.

A **track** has two rails.

9

station

A train stops at a **station**.

People get on. All aboard!

11

wagons

12

This train pulls **wagons**.

passengers

This train carries **passengers**.

express

An **express** train is fast.

hill

A **hill** train is slow.

15

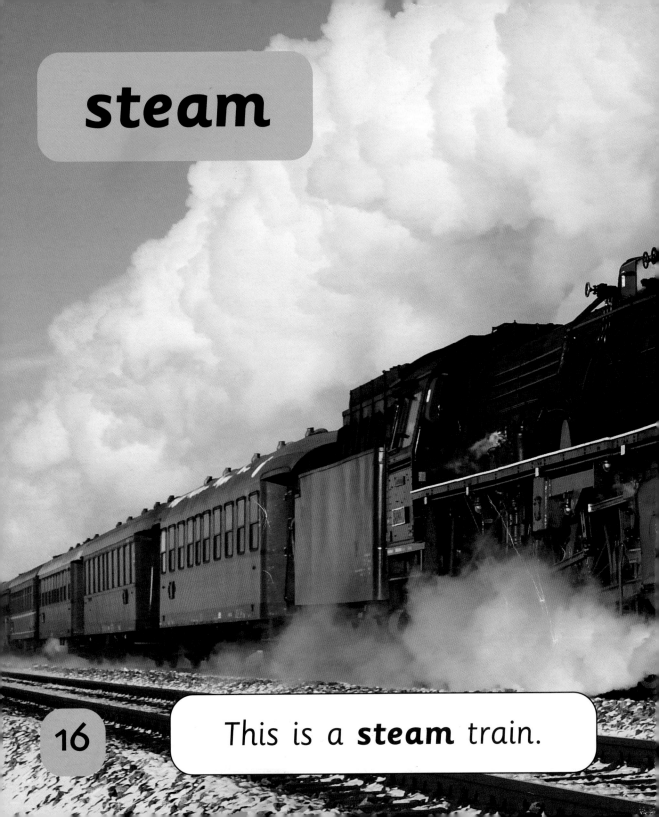

steam

This is a **steam** train.

It has a **steam** engine.

over

This train goes **over** the ground.

18

under

This train goes **under** the ground.

19

What am I?

passengers

driver

wheels

tracks

20

Match the words and pictures.

How many?

Can you count the trains?

21

What noise?

Clickety clack!

Whoosh!

Chuff! Chuff!

Screech!

22

Make a sound like a train!

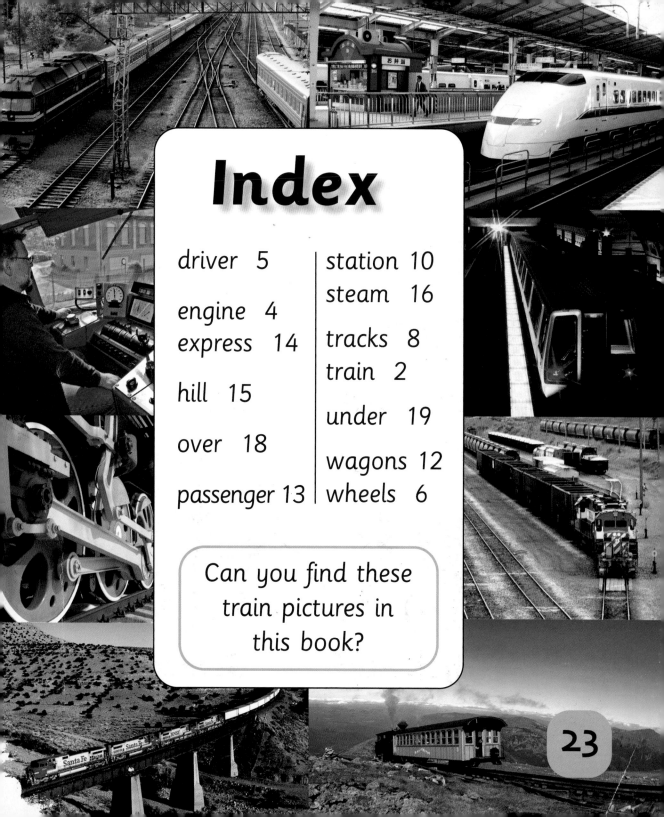

Index

driver 5

engine 4
express 14

hill 15

over 18

passenger 13

station 10
steam 16

tracks 8
train 2

under 19

wagons 12
wheels 6

Can you find these train pictures in this book?

For Parents and Teachers

Questions you could ask:

p.2 What can you see in this picture? Point out the four locomotives in front and line of wagons behind.

p. 4 Why does a train need a strong engine? To pull a heavy load. A locomotive weighs about the same as 50 cars. Some trains are over 4 mi (7 km) long!

p. 5 Would you like to drive a train? Encourage role play: drivers need to know which route they are taking, to follow signals, to stop the train so passengers can get on board, and blow the whistle!

p. 8 How does a train go left or right? You can't steer a train like a car because it runs on tracks. Look at the wheels on page 7. Special switches called points help trains to change tracks.

p. 13 Where can you go on a train? Unlike a car, trains can only travel on tracks. Trains connect big cities as well as smaller towns. On very long journeys passengers sleep on board the train.

p. 15 Why do you think a hill train is slow? Because it has to go up a hill. Most trains travel on flat ground.

When they come to a hill, they go through a tunnel.

p. 16 How can you spot a steam train? Look for the big white clouds of steam coming from the engine and listen for the "chuff chuff" sound.

p. 20 Who am I? If they need a clue, children can look back to pages 5, 6, 8, and 13.

Activities you could do:

• Ask the reader to draw a simple train, writing labels for engine, wheels, wagons, tracks, etc.

• Line up chairs to create a train. Put numbers on the chairs and hand out tickets. You can use props such as suitcases, maps, cap, whistles, etc.

• Ask the reader to describe a train journey they might like to go on, e.g. steam train.

• Introduce trains by reading aloud stories such as *Thomas the Tank Engine, Ivor the Engine,* or *The Little Engine That Could.*

• Show children how to make train whistle sounds by blowing across the top of a plastic bottle.

© Aladdin Books Ltd 2008

Designed and produced by Aladdin Books Ltd

All rights reserved

Printed in the United States

Series consultant Zoe Stillwell is an experienced preschool teacher.

First published in 2008 in the United States by Stargazer Books c/o The Creative Company 123 South Broad Street P.O. Box 227 Mankato, Minnesota 56002

Photocredits: *l-left, r-right, b-bottom, t-top, c-center, m-middle* All photos from istockphoto.com except: 1 , 14, 21 , 22, tl & tr— ALSTOM transport. 2-3, 19, 23mtr & bl—Corbis. 5, 20tl, 23mtl—Andreas Neumann. 18—Flat Earth.

Library of Congress Cataloging-in-Publication Data

Pipe, Jim, 1966-
  Trains / by Jim Pipe.
    p. cm. -- (Read and play)
    Includes bibliographical references and Index.
    ISBN 978-1-59604-165-3
  1. Railroad trains--Juvenile literature. 2. Railroad travel--Juvenile literature. I. Title.

TF148.P56 2007
625.1--dc22

2007007759